Bone Flute

A WOMAN SPEAKS

POETRY

"We leave things at a wild velocity," poet Irene Adler writes in *Bone Flute*, her moving, posthumous collection. In poems that demonstrate an equal tenderness toward life and loss, Adler celebrates the small but profound joys that make any life a miracle in spite of suffering, "black clouds fringed silver." Here, love and sorrow walk hand in hand. Such poems are like a bone flute, one that plays "notes that made a bleak night shine," notes that continue to echo and shimmer in our memory and in the poems found here. Adler plays a fine, sweet music you won't want to miss.

—**Sally Ashton**, author of *Listening to Mars*

Irene Adler's poems are pragmatic, patient, and wily, defiant in their desire for forgiveness and forbearance. With a stark, self-reflexive beauty both airy and earth-bound, Irene's small and sacred meditations reveal what the owls, birds, and beetles already know: life's "wild velocity" lives in every "quill, bone, and feather." As a sister, daughter, and mother, these poems that "sing with delight/for secret reasons" will live in me for a long time.

—**Robin Ekiss**, author of *The Mansion of Happiness*

In this passionate, moving collection, Irene Adler distills a lifetime of asking the big questions into slender lyrics shimmering with longing, grief, and awe. With a delicate sense of music, these poems explore themes of romantic love, familial bonds and trauma, childhood and coming of age, the natural world, and intimations of the divine. In "Genesis," after laying out an alternate cosmology, Adler writes in a line both wry and uncanny, "In the beginning, even God was green." Cleaning voracious pests from her grandmother's garden, her speaker sees not devastation but a vision of ecstasy: "We might all be drowning in roses." The deepest subject of the book is mortality, both that of the speaker and of those she loves, a subject she treats with unsentimental bravery, as in this terse advice from "Heading Home": "leave this life more lightly than / you came and make swift goodbyes." *Bone Flute* is a wise testament to the pain and wonder of being human.

—**Peter Kline**, author of *Mirrorforms*

Bone Flute is a testament to the elegance of the word. Smooth-seeming are the waters into which Irene Adler's words cleanly dive. Through an ease with music and form—from tankas to sonnets—Adler brings a pianist's sensibilities to the page. Her unswerving observations of our human plight surface and surprise again and again: from the humorous ("Above the poet's voice a cry of geese / in flight adds honking to her sonnet.") to the marvelous, through which grief and human desire ("we covet in colors.") entwine and complicate.

—**Cintia Santana**, author of *The Disordered Alphabet*

Bone Flute

A WOMAN SPEAKS

Irene Adler

POETRY

Edited by Angela Narciso Torres

Paloma Press

Copyright © 2025 by The Estate of Irene Adler

All rights reserved. Except for brief passages quoted for review or critical purposes, no part of this book may be reproduced or transmitted in any form or by any means, electronic or mechanical, including photocopying, recording, or by any information storage and retrieval system, without the proper written permission of the copyright owner unless such copying is expressly permitted by federal copyright law. With the exception of nonprofit transmission in Braille, Paloma Press is not authorized to grant permission for further uses of copyrighted selections reprinted in this book without the permission of their owner. Permission must be obtained from the copyright owner as identified herein.

ISBN 9781734496529

Library of Congress Control Number 2025930594

Photos by Alan Adler

Cover Design by Kai Jiang

Printed in the United States of America

PALOMA PRESS
San Mateo & Morgan Hill, California
Publishing Poetry + Prose since 2016
www.palomapress.org

The stumbling out of bed with words
that must be swiftly written down
as if a dam had burst and all the silver
fish must be netted up – or drowned.
But what a thing to start the day
when every fish is found!

"Night Trolling"

Table of Contents

Foreword by Nan Cohen   13

A Note From Alan Adler   17

I.   from *Heading Home*   19

II.   *Yes to the Universe Whatever its Agenda*   27
    White Hyacinths   29
    Memento Mori   30
    Closing the House   31
    Grief   32
    Small Lights in Daily Darkness Are Sometimes
        All We Have of Grace   33
    Miracle   34
    Early and Late   35
    Genesis   36

      *

    First Primer   38
    April   39
    My Daughter's Waterbed   41
    Poetry In Extremis   42
    Ol' Blue   43
    Spring at Filoli   44

      *

    Abigail Adams to John   46
    December   47

Lodestar	48
White Pelicans	49
Coyote, Et Al.	50
Margot Berard	51

III. *After the Unspeakable* — 53

Coloring With Big Sister	55
Childhood I	56
Ego	58
Schadenfreude	59
A Split Second	60
Childhood II	61
Bone Flute	62

*

Losing	64
After	65
At the Golden Gate	66
Casket Room	67
Closure	68

*

Undertow	70
To a Dying Astronomer	73
In the Canal Zone	74
Early Mass	75
Opening the Urn	76
Japanese Beetles	77
Leaving Kauai	78

IV. *Ashes and Bone Bone and Ashes* — 79

Steve Jobs Is Dead, My Daughter Writes	81
[Googling a trip north, an inn]	83
Special Delivery	84

	Ready Aim Fire	85
	Superman	86
	The Amputee	87
	Gravity	88

*

	[The bees are gone.]	90
	Visitation at the Writers' Conference	91
	Feeding Time in the Lion House	92
	Owl	94
	Sidewalk Lizard	95

*

	Prayer	98
	Coming Home	99
	Alzheimer's	100
	Restless Leg Syndrome	101
	Butterflies	102

V.	*The Stuff of Dying Stars*	105
	The Madness of Desire	107
	Lost	108
	Out of Eden	109
	Victorian Red	111
	Remember	112
	Andrew at Ten	113
	A View	114

*

	Sister	116
	The Sunday Dress	117
	Matinee	118
	Harmony	120
	Going Home	121

Afterword	123
Acknowledgments	129
Notes	131
About the Author	135

*

Foreword

Writing her poem "Bone Flute" in 2014, Irene Adler was likely thinking of the nearly complete bird-bone flute excavated in southern Germany in the summer of 2008: "Thirty thousand years along, it still makes / music of breath in a hollowed bone." Such prehistoric flutes have been found in Europe, Asia, and the Americas, fashioned from the bones of vultures, waterfowl, and mammoths.

But whichever real item might have inspired her, Irene approached her subject not as an archaeologist, but as a poet. She imagined both the bone itself and the artifact that some early artist made of it: "Someone heard music in it before / the finger holes were bored…Someone learned to make it sing."

These lines make me think of the writer Irene was then—serious, hardworking, yet not fully convinced that she was a poet. Perhaps she saw herself both in the slender, hollow bird bone waiting to become an instrument, and in the musician who imagined such an instrument into being.

"Bone Flute" is a beautiful, assured poem. In its cadences and imagery one may almost hear the sound of the flute—"notes that made bleak night shine." Any reader would take notice of how, in this and other poems, a sensitive nature is balanced by a keen intellect. And there is also, in the Yeats phrase, "a cold eye": an unflinching, steady awareness of life's pain and losses. (And often with a wonderful dry humor: I'm thinking of the observation, in "The Amputee," that we are all "ortolans / who provide delicacies / for life's French appetites"). "Bone Flute" concludes:

> Found near a grave mound this bone —
> where flower spores still lie
> scattered. Perhaps it was a child.

The grave, the bone flute, the fossilized spores, and the conjectured child: these are powerful juxtapositions, ones which reflect the intensity and delicacy of the work in this collection. Reading *Bone Flute*, we travel with the poet through the seasons of her life, moving through history, through memory, through geography, and yet with a powerful sense of immediacy. Even when the subject of a poem is set many years apart from the speaker's present, the observations feel freshly discovered.

Selected by Angela Narciso Torres with the assistance of fellow poets and editors Naoko Fujimoto and Gail Goepfert from hundreds of poems written by Irene Adler between 1999 and 2023, this collection wisely begins with a brief selection from Irene's privately published chapbook, *Heading Home*—a collection of tanka, written as part of a conversation-in-poems with Angela, in which the poet utilizes the expressiveness and immediacy of this brief form to convey her impressions of nature, time, and feeling as her life draws toward its close. We then continue in reverse chronological order through the archeological layers of Irene's writing—an unconventional but, I think, appropriate way for readers to come to know her as a writer. Her work is interested in what self-discovery and self-revelation are, and these poems demonstrate that these processes are nonlinear and lifelong—they explore the endlessly surprising fluctuations in our knowledge of the self and the world.

I met Irene in 1998 through the poetry writing workshops she took with me in Stanford University's Continuing Studies Program. There, Irene met other Bay Area writers, including Angela, who became a close friend in life and in poetry. After I became poetry director of the Napa Valley Writers' Conference in 2002, Irene and Angela also attended the conference's generative poetry workshops. Over the years in Napa, Irene worked and wrote new poems in workshops with Dorianne Laux, David St. John, Eavan Boland, and Linda Gregerson. One year, Irene gifted the conference a box of flying rings, footballs, and other toys from Aerobie, the company she co-owned and ran with her inventor husband, Alan. For years, these toys were a regular feature of the closing-night picnic (and the company's Aeropress coffee maker remains a necessary fixture in my kitchen). Irene and Alan also regularly and generously donated to the conference's scholarship fund, helping us broaden access for writers who would not otherwise have been able to attend.

Irene continued to take workshops through Stanford Continuing Studies and to befriend other Bay Area poets. In February 2008, she wrote to me, "I'm in two classes at Stanford right now—one on Bach's *Goldberg Variations* and another on poetry with Bruce Snider. My poetry has improved, I think, since last summer. Maybe one day I'll even feel ready to submit something, although people who do tell me it's a depressing process with a lot of rejection. I'd settle for writing things I feel really proud of." Nine years later, she wrote, "I finally submitted a poem and had it accepted"—this was "White Hyacinths," which was published in *RHINO* in 2017.

I am grateful that so much more of Irene's work will be available to readers now, through Alan's steadfast support and Angela's dedication. I feel certain that there are poems here—"Bone Flute," "White Hyacinths," "Sister," "Schadenfreude," "Special Delivery," that will survive the way poems do, lodged like a tough plant in a crack in someone's heart. The real purpose of a book of poetry is to make that happen—that rooting, that unexpected blossom.

Nan Cohen
Los Angeles, February 2025

A Note From Alan Adler

It was my joy to be married to this creative beauty for 61 years. Irene Adler wrote poetry all her life and left the world over 2,000 poems. Here are some of the best, selected by her dear friend, poet Angela Narciso Torres. We hope you enjoy them.

Alan Adler, Inventor
Los Altos, California

I. from *Heading Home*
2021 - 2023

Life was changing; why not writing, too?

—from the author's foreword, *Heading Home*

why do we shun death
trapped in a ruined body
which has done its best
it only means going back
going home with all the rest

*

rivers are rushing
away in April's great flood
and we rush with them
back to the mothering sea
white blood and redheaded home

*

the meaning of life
unknown and unknowable
hovers out of sight
benign as the clear white clouds
icy with indifference

earth will survive us
seas mountains clouds and starlight
rapt in their pulsing
the ageless core still declares
morning again everywhere

*

flaming orange red
the pistache tree leaves flutter
in a last salute
white smoke rides the clean blue air
of a fiery hemisphere

*

more soul than substance
earth's small birds sing with delight
for secret reasons
hawks and eagles never sing
but tear the sky with their cries

in age as in youth
I want never to fail life
while I still have breath
does the hawk refuse to nest
or migrate when the time comes

*

I had a house once
quirky but perfect planted
above the sea where
hawk and meadowlark voices
wove in the song of wild surf

*

the praying mantis
ate a vole at our window
in the dining room
even insects seem to know
how to choose the apropos

loving friends stay so
death will not undo their bond
or drain its comfort
no explanations called for
no need to make amends

*

black clouds fringed silver
swim past while the world's at rest
these eyes miss so much
but trees deserts and mountains
behold the events of night

*

lovers kiss and touch
often and never enough
smiling at themselves
feeling the cold wheeze of death
close in on the ninth decade

poorly slept I lean
into the day's long footsteps
follow patterns there
as I navigate the hours
until the sun rests again

*

smile on a last breath
if you would spite these harpies
surrounding you now
leave this life more lightly than
you came and make swift goodbyes

*

a choir of crickets
vibrates on the summer night
while we search for sleep
how small a thing can guide us
home when we have lost the light

II. Yes to the Universe Whatever its Agenda
2016 - 2020

Yes to the tortoise on whose scored back
The whole cosmos rides to eternity
Yes   And Yes   And indubitably
Yes

WHITE HYACINTHS

These white hyacinths I set beside
your stone could almost raise the dead.

Their scent is such a headiness
I think I hear bones stirring.

Maybe it's wrong to bring the sap of things
so near, risking whatever peace

was made here in a year's seasons.
But gesture is all now. Offerings.

And this is a field that none will reap
except the wind, hungry and sweeping.

MEMENTO MORI

Did you hear the arrow sing
as it left the bow and flew?
Or the sigh of flesh parting?

On a breath the soul escapes
as the pall of death replaces
a vibrancy we knew and prized

skin gone gray and brightness
in the eyes opaque. A spirit
sorely stressed has evanesced.

CLOSING THE HOUSE

It will be like that
things left in order
stopping mail and paper
taking out the trash
heater dialed down
doors and windows tight
setting a light timer
to say someone is home
with you gone away
every room branded
by your choices
and DNA

GRIEF

is that rough gray stone you carry inside
the white ribs of your chest
in bed it tries to smother you
till dawn when you struggle up
and carry it wherever you go.
Breakfast is a plate of bitterness
no matter what.

It never speaks but can be spoken to
lectured, pleaded with, raged against
with no response from a mute tormentor.
Then comes a day when you begin
to notice odd bits of color
enter the dun light of day
and you hate yourself for any
pleasure has become disloyalty
and a stone resents displacement.

SMALL LIGHTS IN DAILY DARKNESS ARE SOMETIMES ALL WE HAVE OF GRACE

smiling at a stranger
over her demanding child,
admiring a couple's new puppy
intent on knotting you in its leash,
helping an old man reach
the applesauce on a high shelf,
courtesy to the caller who thinks
this number belongs to Gladys.

Apologize for the angry
customer who reads out a clerk —
defusing that grenade tossed
at a bruised ego. Allow the other
driver to go first. Stop
without a STOP sign when
someone's family hovers
beside him at the curb.

MIRACLE

A pane of glass separates us
in the arched window beside my bed —
you on an artfully woven nest,
hydrangea hung, I on a mattress.

Jewel on the wing in sunlight —
nest-bound now you warm your eggs —
and when we meet at the window
puzzlement faces delight.

Railroad tracks laid side by side
we spend our odd diurnal lives,
until you migrate in the fall
when I must take your loss in stride.

EARLY AND LATE

Early in love I had to
hug myself to keep the soul
from leaping out of my body —
so wholly unexpected
was the depth of joy
and I so frail a vessel.

Later when a grandchild
died I held myself again
long hours at a time
feeling my heart collapse
at being asked to beat
so mean a rhythm.

Life: what is it you ask of me now?

GENESIS

How did the poet know that rain began
in darkness as the last gasses liquefied.
So many years it took that if the rain
were tears it would have meant a grief
too great for ocean beds to tolerate.
But God, the androgyne, kept weeping
while earth cooled, then solidified,
became a dream incarnate: gauzy
clouds wrapping brown swathes of land
between the sweet, clear blue of seas —
seas yet unsalted by minerals which
later would wash from soil still pristine.
Why did God weep, you want to know?
Was it the birthing of a dream too rich?
A gnawing fear of how all this might go?
In the beginning, even God was green.

Yes to the moons in thrall who must
Tell oceans when to rise and fall
Yes to meteors and fragments unnamed
Yes to comets and gasses and dust
Yes to all stars which shatter and die
Yes though we know not wherefore or why
How dark it would be without their light

"Yes to the Universe Whatever Its Agenda"

FIRST PRIMER

The sea is never still.
It thrives on motion,
will not run out of breath.

Nature's irrepressible child
even at its lowest ebb
shuns sloth and death.

Here endeth the lesson
the wild philosopher read
over a thunderous froth.

APRIL

When spring alters breath
I see a green satin
strapless gown worn by
a young girl poised
on her gray front porch,
rising out of her sheath
like any fresh bloom
breaking away.

Redhaired, with
milky skin that glows
as she descends,
steps into a car,
the boy driving
sober with pride as
they roll toward music
through this quiet,
lush-lawned
neighborhood, going
slowly so folks will
notice his prize
a white gardenia
pinned at her waist,
her hair a ravishment of
copper gold in early
evening light. The low
sun flashes in her green
eyes as she looks sidewise
at him and smiles

that incendiary smile
he will remember long
after the prom.

MY DAUGHTER'S WATERBED

Witness the restoration at night when,
heavy with sleep, she staggers across
the floor to the raft floating there,
settles her body over its amniotic
sea and floats blissfully away from us
dreaming herself buoyant and sleek
at home again in old ocean currents.

Seals at the harbor exist this way
between two elements — awkward
on earth as some adolescents can be
(no thrum of water against the ear
no slip and glide in the sea's embrace),
but suddenly needful of breath and sun
finding the place they're in uneasy.

POETRY IN EXTREMIS

At last I hear the midwife saying:
Yell all you like! and looking closer
I recognize that she is God
who understands as no one can
heroics are greatly overprized.
She is loving. She is wise
and listens as I begin to recite —
softly at first and then louder
until I am shouting through pain
and fear — reaching for affirmation —
the task changed now from torment
to creation and words at a climax
just as the child appears on a gasp
wet eyes blinking with surprise.

OL' BLUE

Rapscallion
Tatterdemalion
Harum Scarum
Hobbledey Hoy

Beggar Master
Feather Disaster
Peanut Blaster
Streetwise Ploy

Neighbor Corrector
Cynic and Lector
Breadcrust Slayer
Poppinjay Boy

SPRING AT FILOLI

Green salvos fired from below
sent up these bugles, their cups
blaring white and yellow Sousa
music — a parade of twirlers
that struts past old magnolias
in white, purple, and rose
strung gray with lichen,
spilling damask petals
slick as a snake's belly.
Fog and clear blue trade places.
Sun and stars, by turns, peek
inside the glass garden house
at two love birds asleep
above pots of narcissus
and hyacinth banked deep
around the cages. The fan-back
chair awaits a breather's swoon.
At the gate someone waves
cars along as if to say, *Go on,
get yourself stunned.* Miles
of oaks later you stagger out,
reading botanical labels
if you can focus, besotted
as a heron stalking stilt-like
in the meadow, unmoved
by the faint of heart.

Yes to the universe and its agenda
Yes to the galaxies in their flight
And to those innumerable stars
Consumed to brighten the way
Yes to planets of every color and size
As they revolve regally or bump along

"Yes to the Universe, Whatever Its Agenda"

ABIGAIL ADAMS TO JOHN

When I lose heart with you, I see
myself moaning there indulgently,
a sight that frightens me more than Hell.

Then the dam of patience breaks,
lashing your face with its icy flood
just as if we had never loved.

I want you to be better than you are,
a less complaining, anger-driven man
who can meet and accept his fate.

On the day they went out of Eden
I suspect Eve took his arm, leaving
the garden, and mentioned a farm.

DECEMBER

In the long darkness, nothing can stanch.
Winter solstice holds its grip on us —
but the knees of crickets begin to itch.

Earth will tilt again on her axis
leaning toward that distant scratch
they must practice, practice, practice.

LODESTAR

In a marriage bed crowded by ghosts
we cling to each other at the edge
they left us, while four parents
criticize the vows we took.

*"With my body I thee worship
and with all my worldly goods
I thee endow..."* they crow, deriding
those sacred words of love.

Our dreams are replays of old
anger, the music of childhood —
the chill of rancor in a house,
the pain of long gray days.

Then I recall my grandmother
who, trapped in some crisis,
bought a new broom to sweep
rooms and staircase clean.

WHITE PELICANS

Aristocrats of air, your landings
smack of novice water skiers —
a gawky yaw, a tardy whoosh
before that barge-like glide of royalty.
Water may be your alter métier,
but the rough transition here
puts hollow bones at risk.
We cringe, watching until
safe to view your placid ride
cloud white to blue on wings like
paddle wheels that lift a dabbler
high again and out of sight.

COYOTE, ET AL.

I heard your call last night
more bark than howl it was
and sent without reply.
But two owls as I
turned out the light
made pure antiphony —
one strong, one soft,
whatever words an owl
might say in darkness.
Coyote trots alone.

The owls will not
renew their messages
or midnight vows
near daybreak with me
tasting the day's air
so near their tree.
What they say is private
and should be
even summer evenings
a cricket's monotony

MARGOT BERARD

after Pierre Auguste Renoir

This holy relic of our love abides
framed above the dictionary stand,
a blue-eyed, wordless child who would
have been a gently ageing bride
long before the Met exhibit you visited
alone in the months of my resistance
to youthful ego and brash speech, to
daily walks you made at dawn for rides
with me, (a car-less ruse) to make amends.
When you unrolled this lovely thing you'd
brought, a token of your better self,
I sensed true worth in an uncertain smile,
and slowly we became close friends.

Her eyes have glowed now half a century
among our books, sweet with yearning
and desire for what she could not say —
but might be written in the pages here.

III. After the Unspeakable
2012 – 2015

you continue this facsimile of
sensate life

a society of others who move and speak
sotto voce

COLORING WITH BIG SISTER

Though it pains me to tell you even now
I was the messy one — smudging lines,
wrinkling pages, pressing so hard
crayons squashed or snapped in two.

Stripes on rabbits, rainbows over heads,
and the unrealistic choices I made —
coloring birds orange because they sang.
Did I mention less than clean hands?

She would press a dent down the center
of our shared bed with her long fingers.
Piano hands, the grownups said. *Artistic.*
Your side, she would say. *Don't cross that.*

But in sleep an arm or foot would somehow
creep and wake me to a sister's hissing.
Trespass of need or only innocence
thorn in an elder sister's suffering side.

CHILDHOOD I

It was a fort with loaded guns aimed
inside at us, the occupants. You could

hear the tick of mines laid underfoot
so we learned to tiptoe quickly room to room.

A closet became our makeshift playpen.
You had to find the string for a light bulb

and never ever pull too soon before
leaving the dolls and kitchen things —

a heavy door that made it hard to hear
that cry when someone lost the knob.

Windows showed the feet of passersby
breaking the light that slanted overhead.

My sister and I learned to knit with nails
and string — copying mother's quick hands —

mine was a draggled tangle, dark with sweat
and torn where I forced the nail head in.

Whatever I made smelled of hot metal,
the sewing stitches full of gray lumps

where I soaped and straightened them.
Grownups went to work and our father

begged for a dollar on his knees
to have "a drink" before his night shift

from four to twelve, not the graveyard
one he was afraid of — wouldn't take.

We wished she would give it to him.

EGO

Such a little word we failed
to see the poison coiled inside.

A vial uncorked from which the genii
slid now running wild

through this his playroom stocked
with atomic toys to fire at will.

My father said if you were reckless
you would doubtless get a bill.

Why does the genie fear to touch
so much that he reviles?

Everyone is running side to side
desperate for a place to hide.

SCHADENFREUDE

A shock greater than the fall   wood
treads raking each vertebra —
was his choked unstoppable laughter
as he picked her up at the bottom —
a collapsed child mass   breath
dispatched   carried her to the couch
and left her there while he opened
the back door to unleash his bass
glee.   Eight and immobilized
she lay gasping in limbo — the living
room a world where father was spelled:
joy-at-another's-harm.   Her harm.
Her father.   The muzzled noise like
an alarm she heard long after his
labored cigarette breathing had stopped.

A SPLIT SECOND

is all it takes for a black hulking
Escalade to meet a Nissan —
ex and im PLOSION. Glass
plastic   steel   shockwaves
crack afternoon apart
and the heart cries: *What is it? Why?*
while clouds drift angelically past
overhead. People stand by
a tall woman who keeps saying
I'm so, so sorry. I really want
her to stop that   or go away.
But this shaking will not.
I watch your left hand fumble
for the driver's door handle   door
without a window. What new ease
of entry this provides.
Ease of exit too. So little fuss.

CHILDHOOD II

> *One of the luckiest things that can happen*
> *to you in life is . . . to have a happy childhood.*
>
> Agatha Christie

Uncle William built a dollhouse for us
his own little girls not yet born.
It was yellow with black shutters and door.
We stood awed in the odor of fresh paint
while mother prompted our thanks. Small
and incautious, I spoke for my big sister
who battled skittishness. Verbal, I spoke
eagerly as I ate: good foods first,
while she, in resignation, ate the worst.

We filled the empty house with what we knew,
shaping clay dishes, rag bag
rugs, table and chairs, a bed or two
from matchsticks, misery, and untamed glue.
In those cellar rooms, in our closet
play space, the yellow shouted out.
I try to go back and change it, to make it right.
But the street is blocked by barricades
stark white in familiar dark.

BONE FLUTE

Someone heard music in it before
the finger holes were bored
lonely for birdsong in the dark.
Someone learned to make it sing.
Thirty thousand years along, it still makes
music of breath in a hollowed bone.
A lost shepherd soothed his flock
blowing its spell over curled wool —
a charm against wolf or blizzard.
The storyteller in a cave might ease
his audience into sleep on stone
with notes that made bleak night shine.
Found near a grave mound this bone —
where flower spores still lie
scattered. Perhaps it was a child.

*the nightmare before you sleep and waking
in its clutch*

*a black well you stand in staring up
at a pinpoint of sky*

*the deaf confessor who nods slyly as your
lips move*

"After the Unspeakable"

LOSING

When the jackpot proves a ruse
When the rains fail and crops sere
When the bride stands alone at the altar
When no one remembers a child's birthday
When the feast is served to empty seats
What has been lost after all?

AFTER

Dry wind blows behind my ribs
where pink flesh should be
and beetles gnaw at fingertips

a carousel of copper bodies
when I turn
as if death were an outing

and I a child wild with excitement
near the band, white
sailboats on a blue pond.

Instead, I'm standing over your
fresh bed, tidying
flowers felled by last night's rain

and my anger fires itself against
the damp adobe soil
that makes your bed.

AT THE GOLDEN GATE

Sunlight or fog, they come to the bridge
                and stand staring down from the ledge

as if tranquility called to them
                blue and faithless, too deep to fathom.

Stepping off, they believe, will cure
                their pain — finally ensure

relief with no thought for that sting
                water commands in parting.

And as their feet leave steel for air,
                survivors say that despair

evaporates, blown on a briny rush
                as if weightless to crush them —

the will to live rises from dread
                to green hillsides, islands spread

on waves, tugboats and cloud billows.
                The heart quickens to a world it knows —

clamors to go back and choose again.
                But gravity beckons the leap of pain

until regret is just a splash in the wide
                surge, a donut of swirl riding the tide.

CASKET ROOM

We hoped for you a house, a wife —
a life of music and family.

But now we choose a polished
maple box for your repose —

a box to fit your recent height
and the ferryman's transit.

The coin in your pocket is twice
the price he is likely to ask —

but you remember how cold
hands grow when rowing —

and we have watched you become
an empathetic fellow who

likes to tip — even the oarsman
for an unanticipated trip.

CLOSURE

Where is the hole I ought to fix
the breach that needs repair?
Walking the fence line I find
no opening   only limitless
miles of barbed wire. Grief
appears to be a walkabout.
A long story that wears out shoes.

I keep hoping for a voice
my weakness for sound paramount.
Is there any way you could signal
from that other side   say
whether it's better now that you've
given up being alive?

You were always easy
at making friends. I count
the possibilities near your marker:
Karen Sue   Jeffrey David   Neil
In thirty-six acres there may be more.
An odd relief to find those names
close by. I talk to them in passing.

what binds us now is a shared thing
outlasting love

a magnet stronger than any blood
brotherhood

"After the Unspeakable"

UNDERTOW

Choking in sea thunder,
your arms thrash against
swells, sandy foam,
the rush of water sucking
you down. Far and farther
away the pale beach with
one striped umbrella –
even the wet black jetty
distant, withdrawn —
your heart applauding
efforts to return,
your ears numb to cries
for help no one hears.

Not fearful, but sad,
and nearly ready to rest,
you see dimly a great
wave rise on a roar —
a bluegreen comma
wearing a white crown.
You spread wide like a
starfish taking a ride
and let the crash push
you closer to land.
Calmer now, you look for
the next aquamarine
train and spread again.

Later will come rest,
ambulance, expensive
tests of heart and lung

scanning for sea water
entry — but you know
now that blood is salt
thrust from a clamoring
heart by its own
ceaseless surges, that
every struggle toward
land becomes an odyssey
eluding known caresses
of undertow and sand.

*

Staying alive requires
air instead of water
for every breath, while
arms and legs push
back at the sucking rush.
You can drown in panic —
a sticky medium where
strength buckles and shreds
the way cardboard folds,
imploding in a warm wash,
its substance sapped
ashen and shapeless,
its threads undone.

Why should we resist
going home at last —
trade a known watery
element for dry
sheets, lumpy bed, that
restless rush of air
when visitors enter — an

uncovered chilly
head to meet death with —
when we could choose
to drift down in gold
flecked gurgling darkness
to the soft sand floor?

*

Open your lips and sip.
Ingest flavors of fish
with preserving salt.
Tip back your head
until ears swim in echoes
seashells often tell.
Now you are adrift —
currents laving your
tired limbs, the sough of
ocean crossed winds
singing you down to rest,
a luminescent grain,
still among zillions.

TO A DYING ASTRONOMER

Heaven lies in a telescope lens
and constellations — that shifting dome
you have so often wandered in
will welcome a devotee. Even
in moonless dark you know
their road signs well.

Would you wait at Orion's belt
for me? My grasp of the seasonal
sky is weak — a small fault
now swollen exponentially
and one thing more to atone for
on a list easy to deplore.

Hoping for a galaxy where
poetry holds sway I stare
over your shoulder as you
unroll star maps for the night's
viewing of long dead lights
but words here are superfluity.

I gaze at that immensity
wishing I understood more
of what your joy was made
straining to see the very core
the universe exploded from as
breadcrumbs to lead you home.

IN THE CANAL ZONE

You lift your Suez eyes and I swim
inside, crossing the isthmus
of you, ocean to ocean. A rush of
waters propels my unplanned
transit past Said and Tawfik
through the Great Bitter Lake
and Africa's languorous sands.

The sun and stars still burn
above but nothing else stays
firm on the Red Sea. My hands
give tremors of desire and deep
in my pelvis something overturns.
Pity me swaying in your near odor
and lash those bluegreen eyes.

EARLY MASS

is in the surge of surf
a body-cooling breeze near dawn
the first ecstasy of bird song,
air pink as blush wine, wafers
of it melting on daybreak's tongue
while the sky blues with beatitudes.

OPENING THE URN

Ashes and grit of white bone I taste
alone   in a private rite
the way a starving person sucks a stone
to give emptiness some ease.

But the taste of you is gone   comfort
has fled as smoke did in billows
from the crematory roof after
your coffin slid inside a door.

Fire finds a voice in the fierce wind
cracking its whip   melting down
what melts and powdering the rest.
Rest seems so needless now.

I try to reverse the film.   Coffin
intact.   Lid prised.   You risen.

JAPANESE BEETLES

Armed with jam jars I harvest
beetles in grandmother's rose garden —
helper and hedonist in a tornado of
copper-green wings and black
wiggly antennae that fondle petals
with delicacy I respect. Even
villains I see can have good taste
in pantry or palette and these are
choosy winged jewels riding the air
heat spawned in a stunning sheen
so much like her porcelain tea set
kept in the English cabinet they were
likely glazed by the same hand.
We might all be drowning in roses.

LEAVING KAUAI

Taking off from this green shimmer across
        a welter of sea
    we watch wing shadows keep

pace with an echo of old volcanic roar.
        Sleeping Giant's
    sharp bones tower and recede

behind a cove where turtles ride waves —
        their copper shells
    and feet caught in every crest.

We leave things at wild velocity
        as if speed itself
    seduces us   not distance

not that bewilderment of light we flee.
        Soaring away
    from this oasis. Strapped in

and resigned to it. Out of sight now
        the westerly island
    in a humpbacked chain   grainy

sand dollar on the brain's atlas. Now
        the water's roiling
    waves us relentlessly away.

IV. Ashes and Bone Bone and Ashes
2005 – 2011

Ashes and bone   bone and ashes
all that lives goes down to dust.
Gold fillings   a wedding ring
memorabilia that will not rust.

STEVE JOBS IS DEAD, MY DAUGHTER WRITES

They haven't said what he died of
yet. He died of life — my dear —
and the cancer — privately
in his own complicated way —
gathered up as all shall be.

Father Time — the Grim Reaper —
Death in his monkish hood — the River
Styx boatman handing him on board
as he does each passenger who comes —
poor or rich — renowned or unknown —
lamented or loathed — ready or not.

Notice how all those symbols of time
and death are male. Curious —
is it not? Death vested in the sex
that mostly plies it. All the great
killers were men: Genghis Khan —
Hitler — Mao — Stalin — millions

and billions of bones interred.
Women populate. Men depopulate.
Now and then a Lucy Borden —
a Boadicea — a Joan of Arc may
rise waving axe or sword.
But mass murderers are men.

Testosterone — the lethal hormone —
brings humankind to grief first

and last. At least Jobs tasted
triumph in his work. His family
must make do with iPhone salutes
and children's sidewalk chalking.

[Googling a trip north, an inn]

Googling a trip north, an inn
pops up, "Clothing Optional."
No worries about what to pack
but a glance at the December
calendar gives pause.

Though even a monk's robe
can be a brown disguise.
What if we could meet old
friends devoid of layers —
see and be seen without
camouflage: Would love
grow more — or less?

A quandary, I confess.
Acceptance is hard enough
without factoring in
tinea versicolor, fat,
birth marks, scars, size,
surprising or otherwise.
Secrets are best kept.

SPECIAL DELIVERY

Death drives up at four in his van
leaving the engine at idle,
takes clipboard and package in hand

and walks past a jungle of camellias
to ring the bell —
waits there, stroking his chin,

while I peer out, then open the door
and greet him like a
welcome suitor. His face is dim

under the cap, eyes shadowed.
But when he offers
me the clipboard to sign, I sense

impatience. It's been a long
day and there's still
this package with its strong

taping to open, its contents
to check and accept.
It would be graceless to resent

a gift which you knew to be
on its way by messenger
whether hemlock,

asp, stroke, or that glitter
of steel in a white
hot flash of cognition.

READY AIM FIRE

Rivers slowly turning red
Gatling and Sten
Smith and Wesson

Winchester
        Winchester
                Winchester

God of the firing pin and stock
Colt or Glock
Remington

Winchester
        Winchester
                Winchester

Drawer and cabinet, rifle rack
hoist your weapon
against attack

Winchester
        Winchester
                Winchester

Safety conquered with a click
stoolies or mobsters
teenage boys

Winchester
        Winchester
                Winchester

SUPERMAN

On the screen Clark Kent
in glasses, suit, and tie, fades out.
Lois Lane or his editor phones
about trouble in Metropolis, making
boyish features wrinkle as he plots —
using the lore of Krypton —
then leaves, to return decked out
in dazzling blue leotard and red
cape, S stamped on a gold diamond.

Raising muscular arms overhead,
he arrows up and flies above the city,
magically, majestically — as mortals
only rise and soar in dreams.
You can breathe again, rattle
popcorn, crush candy wrappers,
glue your gum somewhere and watch
him POW POW and hogtie
villains into growling submission.

Superman, have you retreated
to Krypton? No one here can right
wrongs or quell evil. Trouble
is rife, and peace has so brief
a reign, we go to bed fearful.
How soon will you come back —
restore order, punish the guilty —
sweep down as we dreamed
and carry us to sanctuary?

THE AMPUTEE

Considering lentil versus
minestrone, we met
in a lunch line, me
wrestling my briefcase,
she her crutches and backpack,
ordering sandwiches
as we agreed on French
bread — with anything.

She was young to lose
a leg — I wondered how —
but it hardly mattered.
We're all amputees —
overt or covert parts
lost in passing — ortolans
who provide delicacies
for life's French appetite.

GRAVITY

The creatures we envy most
                are birds, made as they are

to rise and soar   or even dive
                at no cost of earthly law.

*

*Always eager for her own, earth
folds us fast inside her mantle
guardians of organic wealth
whether we die enraged or gentle.*

"Ashes and Bone   Bone and Ashes"

[The bees are gone.]

The bees are gone.
No more golden congregations
around the lavender, no hungry
pulse bumping cestrum flutes or red
tea tree petals. Most of all, I miss
that incessancy, that subsuming of the
one before the many, as if a city
crowded out the individual, drowned
its self-serving cries in a common weal,
commanding the flight to fresh nectar,
the return to fill empty combs.

VISITATION AT THE WRITERS' CONFERENCE

Above the poet's voice a cry of geese
in flight adds honking to her sonnet,
stresses natural as heartbeats
pulsing the lines she speaks
in a classroom ringed by vineyards,
by olive trees shaking their silver
leaves in a rare August shower
that splatters skylights on the roof.

Heads tilt skyward and the room
sways watching this isosceles
migration fly south southeast
to the beat of goose music
quill, bone, and feather plowing
the blue air into furrows.

FEEDING TIME IN THE LION HOUSE

Dazzled as ocean divers
                          by found treasure,
      we open a steel door
                                into noise and light,
            where gates are rising,
                                      inviting cats
to meat-laced cages.

                How stately they enter —

striped Bengal tigers,
                      Siberian whites and
                                  lions who pawed Asia's
        soil before glaciers
                or men
                          drove them south —
claws striding across
                cement as if yellow

grasses were being crushed
                      by emperors passing.

Even the roars have
            fur when they begin
                          battle with their lungs
the musky air thundered
                      into cacophony

roars that shake frail

                biped bodies like

                                rag dolls caught in

      sudden earthquake

                or volcano geyser.

Eyes riveted to steel

            cages, we freeze,

                            arms powerless,

      jaws loose, hearts

                  at flight speed —

thrashing in an ocean

            of old brain echoes —

                          devoured by longing

      for what was lost

                  over a long journey.

We are all stalkers

                and harried prey

      the snarling eaters

                        and the red meat.

OWL

The owl is back —
a stutter of calls
from its dark keep
pulsing the slow
blood of night.

What was numb
begins to stir
eases — lets go.
A withered flame

waxes — rising
higher even than
notes on air
sweetens
tumbled sheets —
pleats the pillow
with a smile.

SIDEWALK LIZARD

You were here first. Before house,
walkway, macadam street you sunned
yourself on granite, whatever held
heat, the kickstart you needed —

you were bigger then, some
long-tailed fellows higher than a house,
gentle browsers like you, but giants —
some with wicked teeth and spines

ate creatures my size for lunch. Now
you live under juniper, a small,
dark comet streaking across
my path to get safe home.

Ashes and bone   bone and ashes
enrich this soil we loved and left
Apples and aspens spring from us
living and dead the warp and weft.

    "Ashes and Bone   Bone and Ashes"

PRAYER

Be kind, Lord. Forgive.
Do not send me back as a tree
to stand patiently, whatever
comes. Nor as a dairy cow
whose task hangs heavier
each sunset, never eased
by the milky mouths.

You know me for tenacity, but
please forbear a cover of shell
and leather skin, a dusty pennant
for a tail — unless passion
might improve desert tortoise
survival rates or shake cactus
needles from this tongue.

Lend me a set of wings instead —
not angel wings of marbled white,
but something fragile, short shrift —
a worker bee's sheer sails
plowing the sunburned air
nectar to hive, folded only as
it dances stories on entry.

Give me a task alone — shoving
a stone up the side of a hill,
hearing it slide back down.
Do not ask why I see turquoise
where others see brown or why
I keep this vigil for an ally
never seen or known.

COMING HOME

The door
opens into
chaos
you must
somehow
navigate
no matter
monsters
no matter what
windowless
room
closes
around you
taboo to speak
taboo to sigh
and thought
so noisy
it gives
you
away

ALZHEIMER'S

You stand there at
                the bottom of the sea,
fathomless weight
                pressing you down as
words bubble past lips
                without sound, your hair
white seaweed lively
                fish dart amidst,
lost shoes and black bag
                sandcast, crab infested,
lined cheeks working
                gill-like to survive
without oxygen the
                steady, oceanic roar.

Up here in a shifting dory
                we peer down through green
water as if you were
                our anchor lost to rust.
We lower gifts of
                lotion, soap, kisses
that fish nibble at until
                they slide along sand
toward a coral burial.
                We watch your hands
groping at silver flashes,
                your lips taking in
deep sips that only
                persist in thirst.

RESTLESS LEG SYNDROME

Sleep, you say, means a night at hard labor —
a pickaxe striking away at scarcity,
the cold stone firing sparks as you lift
and strike — legs twitch, muscles squeal,
bones scream, a syndrome in extreme
that only opioids can slake — or ice
cream. The freezer door opens and closes.
Cookies disappear, wafers at a crowded
Mass, maybe Christmas or Easter Sunday.
Dreams of white pills come earlier each
afternoon as milligrams rise to heights
surprising for one who still walks and talks.

But night sheets thrashing, deep groans,
a voice rasping, *"How long until dawn?"*

BUTTERFLIES

More than a single
generation of monarchs
makes the long migration
down to Mexico. They are
born en route, die,
become replaced. No
Google maps, no name
tags are pinned against
first-day-of-school clothes
no emergency data jingles
on metal neck tags.

Stop signs, left and right
turns, all come encoded,
tucked inside brain
cabinets — in the stem
where the ancient thrives.
Monarchs carry extra
lapidary wing powder
instead of spare tires
and use their company
manners at every stop.
They could use a car hop.

Imagine pursuing a quest
over half a dozen
generations until
it is won. Mother to
daughter, father to son —
grandsons and daughters
carrying a torch still

lighted in storms, a bright
beacon like that light
people who come back
from death tell about.

V. The Stuff of Dying Stars
1999 – 2004

we will scatter our indivisible
bits   the stuff of dying stars
across the universe and a pure
wash of light we lost will cleanse
and heal the shatterings

"After Death"

THE MADNESS OF DESIRE

When I was eight a friend promised me
a chiffon scarf — apricot, like hers.
Every school day I arrived, weak with
appetite for that square of silk as if
it would change my life, remake that drab
basement apartment into a peach seraglio
with all of us in filmy harem pants —
my mother and sister and I asway, smiling,
sinuous, irresistible as cupcakes in a
baker's shopwindow — ecstatically gay.

I learned nothing from brute reality —
the madness of desire still grasps me
periodically, renders me senseless,
pale, importunate, listless to all
but that object meant to erase gray.
It is no accident that Quakers use
gray to calm the fires of earthly desire,
defuse passion, invoke modesty.
We covet in colors: red lips, blue skies,
green Christmas trees, violet eyes.

LOST

We live in the land of lost desires
a fieldstone house with green shutters
open to any ghost who happens by —
or sunlight to raise temperatures.

Quiet descends after dawn
humans stunned by the night,
traffic rerouted and birds gone
in a panic of feathery flight.

OUT OF EDEN

Two went out of Eden
into the land of Nod,
bare shoulders touching

but not holding hands,
not even speaking
eyes on the stony ground.

A desert of silences
hurt their ears used to
birdsong and fresh

waterfalls, the music of
breeze on vine leaves,
the voice of turtles.

But, finally, well past
the gate, they stop,
look around, gaze onto

this vast open plain
barren of green, a lowering
sky, leaden and wide,

pressing them down like
a boulder against sere,
hardscrabble ground.

Their fate smelt of dust,
scorpions — though they must
survive to bear sons

in agony, learn
to scratch sparks of life
from stone, eat insects,

lie down to sleep with no
cover of bush or tree
to shut out the night

and their nakedness,
stung with nettles, always
appeasing God's eyes.

VICTORIAN RED

How many women have worn this ring —
warmed at its banked garnet fire
the color of a hummingbird's throat?

Igneous or metamorphic rock
cradled the stone until a craftsman
cut its facets, polished its gleam

and set it in a filigreed band
three colors of gold — an Italian
sun blazing through the wine.

I think of my mother's appetite for
untouched pages — ten cents a day
novels without a finger smudge.

I prefer antique books with feverish
notes in the margins — ink splatters
where emotion geysered the nib.

I wear old jewelry and rub the stone
as if the genie inside might rise
like a giant teardrop and tell

its history of imprecations,
its sequence of female possessors,
its lost pledges of fidelity.

REMEMBER

Remember when we had so much to say
that there were no days long enough
to say it in — and only small rests
between caresses — with time apart spent
in conversation about the absent other —
or dreaming of our last or next encounter?
We shared a narrow bed. It did not matter.
With colds or flu we kissed, nonetheless.

There was a moment once after passion
when I understood the threat of death
had flown — had lost its power to cheat
as it might have had I never known
bone throbbing, skin singeing breaths
from your mouth to mine. Epiphany.

ANDREW AT TEN

Too shy to speak, he rang
our bell and stepped into
a field of snow beside
the door, his marzipan
gift sugared with white
crystals as they fell
amidst furred stillness.

We were ten that Christmas.
Andrew, in my class
at school, stared daily
from round pools of blue
above a gapped smile.
His spiky yellow hair
was not then in fashion.

The Jameses kept horses
and he moved in an
aura of their smell.
His silent deeds of hope
embarrassed and displeased
because my friends and family
teased me endlessly.

Too late I grew
wise enough to cherish
worship and the sturdy
clop of barn boots
outside a winter door.
How little we know of love
left by starlight.

A VIEW

Three redwood trees
scabrous with some new
disease, a pale, late
day gibbous moon
with stratus in between.
A view is all we have
sometimes — roof top
tilted, sucking us high
up into blue ether
as if we could breathe
better away from here —
but for these magnetized
shoes, earth crusty,
clinging to stones and bone.

*we two sisters will boycott
Paradise   fall through infinite
blue space and never meet
again what bred us in bitterness.
Wait for me until I come.*

"After Death"

SISTER

You are my black hole in the universe
which now sucks vertiginous into
its maw of space whatever circles near
thoughts, odors, images of you
in place on earth before this sudden
absence erased your raised left brow,
that low chuckle with which you met fear
and ten slender fingers chattering.

What was left of you after the cancer
they set afire in our mother's zeal
to outface nothingness. Only the air
holds a trace of iris, cortex,
vein — and I walk in rain as it drops
particles of things you shed, hoping
for some thunderclap to strike
meaning from this dull anvil of pain.

THE SUNDAY DRESS

He always hit us on the head —
calloused palm at waist height
scything the air back like an engine
steaming fast on a curved track.

That hand flung my sister's honey-
colored head against the wall
in grandmother's hall making
a calamitous thunk.

Three-thousand miles and years away
I hear that sound, wondering why
we never spoke of those roundhouse blows —
even after father was dead.

Oh, Theodore! my grandmother cried.
Hers were the only tears shed.
My sister slid against the wall and sat,
thin legs splayed on dark carpet.

Modesty paralyzed, she stared
down at two white outrageous
thighs until a hand, slow motion,
smoothed her blue Sunday dress.

MATINEE

Breathless and tired from hurrying,
we dropped into front row
seats as credits unreeled.
Was that the critical mistake?
Slowly I became aware that you
were making a great snore —
your head thrown back against
the plush theater seat, eyes
all white — what I could see,
at least — hands hanging down.

We settled down and a dark
mountain rose between us
that I couldn't get through,
The soundtrack and I both
failing to wake you. I crept
up the aisle to an usher, hoping
you'd call me back: *Grandmother
fell asleep and she won't wake up.*
Words brought tears he
left me wiping while he ran for
manager, telephone, ambulance —
a stretcher crowding the dark air
as scenes on the screen above
passed in erratic flickers.

You lay silent now under that
gray blanket. They would not
let me take your hand, but I
was beside you, a walk-on in this
drama until my mother should arrive

from work on Park Avenue, blaming
me for reasons I never could
predict — quick, scolding, angry —
renewing her firm belief that life
would always bring her grief, though
you were not her mother
and father saw us all as enemies.
Outside, the sky was white with heat,
the street black, aroil with traffic,
passersby curious, craning, quick
sympathy in the air — a child
who drank it like lemonade — and a
slim, dark-haired woman nearly
running along Front Street toward
The Sign of the Ram marquee.

HARMONY

We used to sing together,
my sister Kay and I.
It was the only thing
we did in harmony
with Dad, who whistled
while we took parts
hers alto melody,
mine the higher line.

It would start by
chance in the kitchen
each of us, leaning
against tabletop
or cabinet, not
looking much at each
other, just shaping
the notes to intertwine.

Three myopic spiders
might spin that way,
from separate corners,
a sticky silk thread
sailing out to clasp
lines from the other
two scarcely seen
partners in the web.

GOING HOME

Light slips between the trees
at six — that hour of going home —
when snails lay sticky tracks
to beat the sun, when raccoons,
skunks and possums seek nests
against diurnal predators,
herding their young into storm
drains, attics and rank ditches.

I wave them on, witnessing
that oldest of migrations —
going home. Home to shelter,
friendly smells and cool in heat —
home to sympathy, caresses
and a curl of space to rest.

Afterword

On June 28, 2023, four months before Irene Adler left the world she loved, she wrote me:

> *Yesterday in our clear blue skies I watched the wild up-rushing wind exciting the young, young trees as if the spirits of life could hardly contain themselves. What was it Hopkins said—'All that juice and all that joy!' I am drifting away but joy, that is eternal . . . Every day I rise to see what the world is doing!*

Despite a two-year struggle with the cancer that claimed her in October 2023, Irene's voice carried that unfailing wonder and excitement of being in the world—"the glory and pain and mystery of it." It was the same voice I knew and loved throughout twenty-three years of friendship, beginning with a poetry workshop taught by Nan Cohen through Stanford's Continuing Studies Program in 2002.

A rare thing sometimes happens in a writing workshop. Someone's poems strike a chord, and somehow you know you'll remain friends long after. Despite our age difference—I, then a young mother of boys, and Irene, a retired high school teacher from Palo Alto—were soulmates from the start. Our friendship grew from a shared love of poetry but went well beyond. Over the years, we took several classes with Stanford CSP's illustrious faculty—Robin Ekiss, Bruce Snider, Peter Kline; at the Napa Valley Writers' Conference; and later with Sharon Olds, Ellen Bass, Dorianne Laux, and Sally Ashton. We formed a monthly peer workshop with fellow Bay Area poets. Irene continued to host poetry workshops at her home for many years.

Irene and I had a long-standing ritual of meeting over lunch to discuss writing and life—children, grandchildren, marriage, ailing parents, music, gardening, climate change, and more. The ritual often ended with a bookstore run to browse the latest books from poets we admired: Sharon Olds, Jane Hirshfield, Jack Gilbert, Mona Van Duyn, Linda Pastan, Seamus Heaney, Li-Young Lee. Our shelves looked strikingly similar.

Like Didion, Irene wrote "to find out what I'm thinking, what I'm looking at, what I see and what it means." Like Plath, writing was her way of "ordering and reordering the chaos of experience." Her poems sought to "praise the mutilated world," as Zagajewski's poem goes. In a 1999 journal entry, she writes "Poems keep coming and make me delirious with joy . . . I don't think I could live anymore without writing."

When Irene's husband Alan asked me to edit a collection of her poetry, it was not without warning about the enormity of the task. She left over two thousand poems from the late nineties to 2023, rarely seeking publication despite encouragement from those who knew her work's merit. As poet Sally Ashton said, "Irene wrote to write, but her work deserves to be read."

Fellow *RHINO* editor-poets Gail Goepfert and Naoko Fujimoto helped me organize, read, and cull poems for the manuscript. My son Timothy, a computer programmer and emerging poet, coded a program to narrow the pool to 1,770 discrete files, grouping poems with earlier versions when possible. Though Irene and I exchanged poems for decades, many of these I was seeing for the first time. I sometimes felt I was getting to know her more deeply than in her life. She once wrote in a letter, "Maybe poems are the truest things we say to each other."

Using the rigorous criteria and rating system we employed at *RHINO*, my co-editors and I agreed to select only poems that required minimal editing, if any. Each poem received at least two readers before the final selection. Since Irene regarded many of these as drafts, it was important to use the highest standards, guided by my years of workshopping with Irene and an intuitive sense of what she would consider finished.

The decision to present the poems in reverse chronological order was borne out of a desire to recreate the experience of meeting Irene for the first time, gradually peeling back layers as one does with a new acquaintance. A poet's development is often circuitous. Themes are revisited and ideas tested again and again, yielding new discoveries. For Irene, reinvention and revision were constants in the attempt to say something true.

Each of the book's five sections is introduced with a poem from the author as an organizing insight for the poems that follow. This epigraph poem is given in parts, each beginning a subsection while providing a unifying thread. Like *amuse-bouchées* served between courses, these breaks refresh, awaken, and offer glimpses of the poet's hand: her presence in absence.

An overarching goal was to represent Irene's mastery as well as her boundless curiosity. Irene was a master of lyricism, rhetoric, and form. Inspired by Bishop and Dickinson, her poems covered the ephemera of life, the rewards of attention, the wonders and sorrows of being alive. There are poems that lament environmental collapse, the political chaos of the times, the cost of technological advancement in human connection. Her poems reflect on the afterlife, work through childhood wounds, honor friendships, and sing of hearth and home. When a grandson died unexpectedly in 2012, poetry helped Irene make sense of that unfathomable loss, giving rise to some of her best poems. Several appear in these pages.

Sixteen months after a large box of poems arrived at my doorstep, we have this debut collection representing over two decades of Irene Adler's poetry. Only the laxest generosity has made this miracle possible. My deepest gratitude goes to Aileen Cassinetto of Paloma Press for believing in this project from the start; to my co-editors and friends Gail Goepfert and Naoko Fujimoto for their collaboration and support; to Timothy Torres for many hours of technical and editorial assistance. Huge thanks to cover designer Kai Jiang for her vision and artistry. Immense gratitude to Nan Cohen for her encouragement, wisdom, and friendship. Endless thanks to Alan Adler, without whose energy and vision this book would not have been born.

Recently, I stumbled upon this letter in which Irene recounts a dream about one of her favorite poets, Emily Dickinson. What better way to close than with these words, which reflect on the abiding spirit that infuses so much of Irene's poetry:

> *I woke this morning murmuring, and Alan asked if I were speaking to him. But it was Emily Dickinson I was speaking to. "A narrow fellow in the grass occasionally rides..." Her words seem so fresh after a couple of centuries. Did she wake up with words? We know she percolated them through the day while she did ordinary things. I so wish she could know how much those words mean to me and to uncounted numbers of people for whom she spoke. Her passion and abiding love for the natural world fairly leaped from her pen, pencil - whatever scrap she had nearby to get the words down on. But so few people valued the poems she wrote while she was alive.*
>
> *Since her death, of course, she has become a beacon to people like me in other centuries. Our worlds differ in so many ways - but not in that deeper understanding of what it is to be human, to wonder at earthly life, to live it without knowing why. And then to yield it up in a disconnection we cannot fathom. Words are the poultice we use to ease both joy and sorrow. We are made to love wholly - without wholly understanding. And she speaks for us in cadences that accept and honor the mystery. Shakespeare says we owe God a death. We also owe poets a debt for their voices, especially those who had no acclaim. Maybe clouds are the best poetry - endlessly, marvelously reinvented and outlasting all voices.*
>
> *Sometimes I wonder what will happen to all [these] pages of poetry. It could make an enlightening display, a windblown letter to the world. A kind of praise.*

It's been my great honor and privilege to serve as the courier for Irene's windblown letter to the world. I can think of no higher tribute to a fellow sojourner in poetry and in life. I am certain that, like the bone flute, these poems will continue to sing throughout the ages.

Angela & Irene, 11 July 2014

Angela Narciso Torres
February 15, 2025
Oceanside, California

Acknowledgments

"White Hyacinths," p. 29, first appeared in *RHINO* 2017 (rhinopoetry.org/poems/white-hyacinths-by-irene-adler).

"Spring at Filoli," p. 44, "White Pelicans," p. 49, "[The bees are gone]," p. 90, "Owl," p. 94, and "Butterflies," p. 102, first appeared in *The Nature of Our Times: Poems on America's Lands, Waters, Wildlife, and Other Natural Wonders* (natureofourtimes.poetsforscience.org/tag/irene-adler/).

Notes

1. "Life was changing – why not writing, too?" p. 19. *Heading Home* is a privately published tanka collection Irene wrote between 2021-2023. In the preface, Irene writes:

> *In December of 2021, I was given a diagnosis of a rare cancer that quickly became metastatic. While exploring options, which proved fruitless, a dear friend and fellow poet, Angela Torres, sent me some tanka and suggested we exchange work in that form.*

> *The challenge of a new form appealed to me. Life was changing – why not writing, too? But I had no idea at the beginning how supportive and sustaining this new challenge would become. My gratitude for the suggestion and the exchanges is boundless.*

> *Now, nearly halfway into 2023, I am still writing tanka and printing samples to let people know how, in part, I have spent the last 16 months. Tanka, a venerable Japanese form of poetry, is written in an American voice in these pieces. I encourage anyone interested to explore the oldest examples of tanka writing, as mysterious and beautiful as life itself.*

2. "Spring at Filoli," p. 44. Irene and Alan often visited the Filoli gardens surrounding the 1917 brick Georgian mansion. Originally built as a private residence in Woodside and opened to the public in 1975, "the estate boasts 654 acres of beauty nestled along the slopes of California's coastal range. The property is considered one of the finest remaining country estates of the 20th century." (from www.filoli.org)

Photo courtesy of Alan Adler

3. "White Pelicans," p. 49. The heaviest of North American birds, American white pelicans visit the San Francisco Bay Area every summer.

4. "Margot Berard," p. 51. This famous Renoir painting, in view at the New York Met, depicts the five-year-old daughter of Renoir's devoted patron Paul Berard, a diplomat and banker whom he met in 1878. A reproduction of the painting was the first gift Alan gave Irene during their courtship. Alan recalls how Irene loved this painting so much so that she had it framed even when she could ill-afford it at the time. The framed print hangs over the dictionary stand in their home, still in its original frame.

Photo courtesy of Alan Adler

5. "Childhood l," p. 56. Irene's father Theodore, an alcoholic, was verbally and physically abusive to his two daughters, often threatening to kill them.

6. "A Split Second," p. 60, refers to an accident in which Irene's Nissan was rear-ended by a huge black Cadillac Escalade, sending her to the hospital.

7. "[the bees are gone.]," p. 90. Irene and Alan loved bees, often observing them in their flower-filled backyard in Los Altos where Alan enjoyed photographing them. This poem may be referring to colony collapse disorder or the seasonal disappearance of thousands of bees during the Bay Area's winter months.

8. "Bone Flute," p. 62. In 2009, Irene and Alan read with enthusiasm about the scientific discovery by German researchers of Paleolithic flutes crafted from hollow bone. Alan, an American inventor with over forty patents, has made and played end-blown flutes for most of his life. Irene often helped him refine the timbre of his flutes, which often employed the same principle of tone creation as these ancient instruments.

Our gratitude to Alan Adler for contributing information and photographs to some of these notes.

Irene Adler was a poet and English teacher in Palo Alto, California, where she was also a co-owner of the company that invented the Aerobie flying ring and the Aeropress coffee maker. By the time of her death in October 2023, she had written over 2,000 poems spanning 25 years.

*Worse than a bump in the night is none
finding ourselves alone in the stillness
adrift in the wider universe*

www.ingramcontent.com/pod-product-compliance
Lightning Source LLC
Chambersburg PA
CBHW060613080526
44585CB00013B/811